Home Biz Ideas to Launch Now

Maximize Earnings and Flexibility with These Home Business Concepts

Alex Brightwealth

Contents:

Freelance Services: Offer services like writing, graphic design, web development, or social media management

Online Tutoring: Teach subjects you're knowledgeable in via video conferencing

E-commerce Store: Sell products on platforms like Etsy, eBay, or your own website

Virtual Assistant: Deliver organizational and administrative aid to companies from a distance

Blogging or Vlogging: Share your expertise or passion through written articles or videos

Fitness Coaching: Offer virtual fitness training sessions or create personalized workout plan

Cooking/Baking: Sell homemade meals, baked goods, or cooking classes online

Digital Marketing Consultancy: Help businesses improve their online presence and marketing strategies

Online Coaching: Offer life coaching, career guidance, or personal development services

Handmade Crafts: Create and sell crafts, jewelry, or art through online marketplaces

App Development: If you have coding skills, create and sell mobile apps

Pet Services: Offer pet sitting, dog walking, or grooming services

Online Reselling: Source and sell products from thrift stores or wholesalers on platforms like Amazon

Gardening/Landscaping: Provide gardening advice, plant sales, or landscape design services

Home Cleaning Services: Offer cleaning and organizing services to local clients

Tech Support: Provide technical assistance to individuals or small businesses remotely

Virtual Event Planning: Help plan and coordinate virtual events, conferences, or workshops

Personal Styling: Offer fashion advice and styling services through virtual consultations

Freelance Services: Offer services like writing, graphic design, web development, or social media management

In the ever-evolving landscape of modern business, the freelance economy has emerged as a thriving avenue for professionals to offer specialized services to a diverse range of clients. From crafting compelling narratives to building captivating visuals, freelancers in fields such as writing, graphic design, web development, and social media management play a pivotal role in meeting the needs of businesses worldwide. This chapter explores not only the services themselves but also provides a guide on how to get started in each of these freelancing niches.

Skill Assessment and Specialization:
Begin by evaluating your skills and interests. Identify your strengths and decide on the specific services you want to offer within the freelance realm. Consider your expertise in writing, graphic design, web development, or social media management and choose one or a combination based on your strengths.

Branding and Niche Selection:
Craft a unique brand identity that reflects your style and expertise. Choose a business name, design a professional logo, and create a cohesive visual presence across your online platforms. Select a niche within your chosen field (e.g., tech-focused writing, minimalist graphic design, e-commerce web development, niche-specific social media management).

Portfolio Creation:
Even if you're just starting out, create a portfolio showcasing your best work. If you don't have client projects to display, consider creating mock projects that demonstrate your skills. This will help potential clients gauge your abilities and style.

Setting Rates and Packages:
Research the going rates for your services within the industry and adjust based on your experience and skill level. You can offer different packages at various price points to cater to different client needs. Make sure your rates reflect the value you provide.

Build an Online Presence:
Create a professional website that showcases your portfolio, services, rates, and contact information. Consider starting a blog or sharing informative content related to your field to showcase your expertise and attract potential clients.

Networking and Marketing:
Utilize social media platforms, forums, and online communities relevant to your niche to connect with potential clients. Engage in discussions, offer helpful advice, and share your work to establish yourself as an expert. Participate in industry events, both online and offline, to expand your professional network.

Outreach and Client Acquisition:
Start by reaching out to your existing network, family, and friends for referrals and potential clients. Craft personalized pitches and proposals for businesses that align with your services. Highlight how your expertise can solve their specific challenges.

Deliver Exceptional Work:
When you secure your first clients, ensure you deliver high-quality work on time. Exceed their expectations and maintain open communication throughout the project. Positive client experiences can lead to repeat business and referrals.

Testimonials and Reviews:
As you complete projects, request feedback and testimonials from satisfied clients. Display these on your website and marketing materials to build trust and credibility with potential clients.

Continuous Learning and Improvement:
Stay up-to-date with the latest industry trends, tools, and technologies. Invest in continuous learning to enhance your expertise and provide innovative solutions to clients.

Scaling and Diversifying:
As your freelance business grows, consider hiring subcontractors or collaborating with other freelancers to take on larger projects. Explore expanding your service offerings based on demand and industry trends.

Remember, establishing a thriving freelance enterprise requires time and unwavering commitment. Consistency, professionalism, and a passion for delivering value to your clients will set you apart in this competitive landscape.

Online Tutoring: Teach subjects you're knowledgeable in via video conferencing

In the digital age, the landscape of education has expanded beyond traditional classrooms. Online tutoring has emerged as a powerful platform for sharing knowledge and helping students succeed. By leveraging the convenience of video conferencing, tutors can provide personalized learning experiences that cater to individual needs. This chapter delves into the world of online tutoring, exploring its benefits, strategies for success, and how to get started in this rapidly growing field.

Identify Your Expertise:
Identify the subjects you possess knowledge and passion for. These could range from academic subjects to specialized skills like music, languages, coding, or test preparation.

Define Your Target Audience:
 Decide on the age group, educational level, and demographic you want to tutor. Tailoring your approach to a specific audience can help you connect better with your students.

Curriculum and Content Creation:
Develop a structured curriculum or lesson plan for each subject you'll be tutoring. Create engaging materials such as presentations, worksheets, quizzes, and interactive exercises that cater to different learning styles.

Choose a Platform:
Select a reliable video conferencing platform for your tutoring sessions. Consider options like Zoom, Skype, Google Meet, or specialized tutoring platforms that offer tools for scheduling, recording sessions, and screen sharing.

Set Your Rates:
Research the market rates for online tutoring in your subject area and decide on competitive pricing. You might offer different pricing tiers based on session length or package deals.

Build a Professional Online Presence:
Create a professional website or landing page that showcases your expertise, services, rates, and testimonials from satisfied students. Your website should reflect your teaching style and values.

Marketing and Branding:
Develop a unique brand identity for your online tutoring business. Use social media, educational forums, and online communities to promote your services. Share valuable educational content and engage with potential students.

Create Engaging Promotional Content: Develop engaging content such as video lessons, blog posts, or social media posts that demonstrate your teaching style and approach. Highlight your expertise and how you can help students succeed.

Offer Free Workshops or Webinars:
Host free webinars or workshops on topics related to your tutoring services. This can help you showcase your teaching skills, build your audience, and establish credibility.

Personalized Assessments:

Offer free initial assessments to understand the student's level and learning needs. This will allow you to tailor your tutoring sessions to their specific requirements.

Interactive Sessions:

During tutoring sessions, make use of interactive tools like virtual whiteboards, screen sharing, and collaborative documents to enhance the learning experience.

Provide Regular Feedback:

Regularly evaluate your students' advancement and offer constructive input. Celebrate their accomplishments and address areas for enhancement.

Flexible Scheduling:

Provide flexible scheduling choices to accommodate students' busy schedules. Consider time zone differences if you're tutoring students from around the world.

Engage Parents (For K-12 Tutoring):

Maintain open communication with parents about their child's progress through regular reports. Maintain open communication channels to address any concerns they might have.

Continuous Learning:

Stay updated with the latest educational trends and teaching methods. This will help you provide the most effective and relevant instruction to your students.

Collect Testimonials:
Solicit feedback and endorsements from content students and parents. Display these on your website and marketing materials to build trust and attract new clients.

Starting an online tutoring business requires patience, dedication, and a genuine passion for education. Providing a personalized and supportive learning environment will help you stand out and create a positive impact on your students' educational journey.

E-commerce Store: Sell products on platforms like Etsy, eBay, or your own website

The digital age has ushered in a new era of commerce, where entrepreneurs and artisans can reach global audiences with the click of a button. E-commerce stores have become a cornerstone of modern business, offering a platform to sell products on platforms like Etsy, eBay, or one's own website. This chapter delves into the world of e-commerce, unveiling the strategies, benefits, and essential steps to thrive in this dynamic marketplace.

Choose Your Niche:
Decide on the type of products you want to sell. Focus on a specific niche that aligns with your interests, expertise, and market demand. This will help you stand out and cater to a targeted audience.

Research and Validate:
Conduct comprehensive market research to comprehend your target demographic, their preferences, and purchasing behaviors. Validate your product ideas by assessing competition, demand, and potential profitability.

Business Plan:
Develop a comprehensive business plan that outlines your niche, target market, competitive analysis, sourcing strategies, pricing, and marketing approach. This plan will serve as your roadmap.

Sourcing Products:
Decide whether you'll create your own products, source from manufacturers, or use dropshipping. Ensure the quality of your products and maintain consistent inventory.

Branding and Store Name:
Select a distinctive and unforgettable name for your online store. Create a brand identity that reflects your niche and resonates with your target audience.

Design Your Store:
 Create an appealing and user-friendly online store. Choose an e-commerce platform like Shopify, WooCommerce, or BigCommerce to set up your store. Customize the layout, colors, and imagery to align with your brand.

Product Listings:
Write compelling product descriptions that highlight the features, benefits, and unique selling points of each item. Use high-quality images to showcase your products from different angles.

Pricing Strategy:
Determine your pricing strategy by considering factors like product cost, competition, and perceived value. Don't forget to factor in shipping costs and fees associated with the e-commerce platform.

Set Up Payment Gateways:
Choose reliable payment gateways that offer secure and seamless transactions. Consider options like PayPal, Stripe, or credit card payments.

Shipping and Fulfillment:
Decide on your shipping methods and rates. Offer options like standard, expedited, or international shipping. Ensure timely completion of orders to uphold customer satisfaction.

Customer Service:
Provide exceptional customer service by promptly responding to inquiries, addressing concerns, and offering assistance. Favorable interactions can result in recurring business and recommendations.

Marketing Strategy:
Develop a marketing plan that includes social media marketing, content creation, email marketing, influencer collaborations, and paid advertising. Tailor your strategy to your target audience and chosen platforms.

Launch Promotion:
Build excitement for your store launch with a special promotion or giveaway. Harness your social media presence and interact with prospective clients.

Monitor Analytics:
Use tools like Google Analytics or e-commerce platform analytics to track website traffic, sales, and customer behavior. Adapt your approaches based on insights from collected data.

SEO Optimization:
Enhance your product listings and website for better search engine visibility. Use relevant keywords, meta descriptions, and alt text for images to improve visibility in search results.

Content Creation:
Regularly update your store with fresh content, such as blog posts, videos, or product spotlights. This not only engages customers but also enhances your website's SEO.

Customer Feedback:
Encourage customers to leave reviews and testimonials. Positive reviews establish trust and credibility among potential purchasers.

Adapt and Grow:
Continuously analyze your results, adapt your strategies, and expand your product offerings based on customer feedback and market trends.

Starting an e-commerce store requires dedication, creativity, and ongoing effort. Providing a seamless shopping experience, valuable products, and excellent customer service will help you build a loyal customer base and establish a successful online business.

Virtual Assistant: Deliver organizational and administrative aid to companies from a distance

In today's fast-paced business landscape, the demand for flexible and remote support services has given rise to the virtual assistant industry. Virtual assistants (VAs) deliver invaluable organizational and administrative aid to companies from a distance. This chapter is your compass to understanding the dynamic world of virtual assistance, offering insights into the role, benefits, strategies, and steps to excel in this burgeoning field.

Identify Your Skill Set:
List the administrative and organizational skills you excel in, such as scheduling, email management, data entry, social media management, or bookkeeping.

Define Your Services:
Determine the specific virtual assistant services you'll offer. You could specialize in a niche like real estate, e-commerce, coaching, or digital marketing.

Research Your Target Market:
Identify the types of businesses or individuals that could benefit from your services. Tailor your services to address their requirements and challenges.

Create a Brand Identity:
Choose a business name that reflects your services and create a professional logo. Craft a clear mission statement and values that resonate with your potential clients.

Set Up Your Workspace:
Create an organized and efficient workspace in your home. Invest in the necessary tools, software, and equipment to provide top-notch virtual assistance.

Develop Service Packages:
Design service packages with different levels of support and pricing. This allows clients to choose a package that matches their requirements.

Build an Online Presence:
Create a user-friendly website showcasing your services, pricing, testimonials, and contact information. Optimize your website for search engines to attract potential clients.

Content Marketing:
Start a blog or create informative content related to virtual assistance and business productivity. Share tips, guides, and industry insights to position yourself as an expert.

Networking:
Join online business communities, social media groups, and platforms like LinkedIn. Engage with potential clients, share your expertise, and build relationships.
Portfolio and Case Studies:

As you gain clients, create a portfolio showcasing successful projects and case studies. Highlight how your assistance positively impacted their businesses.

Pricing Strategy:
Set competitive rates based on your experience, skill level, and the services you provide. Consider offering different pricing models, such as hourly, project-based, or retainer.

Outreach and Proposals:
Initiate contact with potential customers via email or social platforms. Craft personalized proposals that address their specific pain points and explain how your services can solve them.

Client Onboarding:
Develop a smooth onboarding process for new clients. Clearly communicate your services, expectations, and communication methods.

Time Management:
Implement effective time management techniques to juggle multiple clients and tasks efficiently. Utilize tools like task management apps to stay organized.

Communication Skills:
Maintain open and clear communication with your clients. Respond promptly to emails, messages, and inquiries.

Upselling and Cross-Selling:
As you build relationships with clients, identify additional ways you can support them. Offer complementary services or suggest upgrades to their existing packages.

Continuous Learning:
Stay abreast of current industry trends, software, and tools. Continuously broaden your skill set to offer a more extensive array of services.

Client Satisfaction:
Regularly check in with clients to ensure they're satisfied with your services. Address any concerns promptly and make necessary adjustments.

Referrals and Testimonials: Encourage satisfied clients to refer you to their contacts and leave testimonials. Favorable verbal recommendations can greatly enhance your business.

Scale Your Business:
As your client base grows, consider hiring additional virtual assistants to help with workload. This allows you to take on more clients and expand your services.

Starting a virtual assistant business requires a combination of organization, communication skills, and a proactive mindset. Providing reliable support and efficient solutions will position you as a valuable partner for businesses seeking remote assistance.

Blogging or Vlogging: Share your expertise or passion through written articles or videos

In the digital age, sharing knowledge, expertise, and passions has taken center stage through the mediums of blogging and vlogging. Whether through written articles or captivating videos, individuals have the opportunity to connect with global audiences, foster communities, and even transform their hobbies into successful ventures. This chapter delves into the exciting realms of blogging and vlogging, offering insights into the significance, strategies, and key steps to embark on this creative journey.

Discover Your Passion:
Identify a topic you're passionate about and knowledgeable in. Whether it's travel, cooking, technology, fashion, or personal development, your enthusiasm will shine through in your content.

Narrow Your Niche:
Delve deeper into your chosen topic to find a unique angle or sub-niche that sets you apart from others. For example, if you're into travel, you might focus on sustainable travel tips or off-the-beaten-path destinations.

Craft Your Brand:
Develop a clear brand identity that reflects your style and message. Choose a memorable name, design a logo, and create a consistent visual aesthetic across your content.

Content Strategy:
Plan the type of content you'll create, whether it's written articles, videos, or a mix of both. Develop a content calendar to ensure regular and consistent updates.

Storytelling:
Infuse your content with storytelling elements. Share personal anecdotes, experiences, or challenges to make your content relatable and engaging.

Create High-Quality Content:
Prioritize quality over quantity. Whether you're writing articles or filming videos, invest time in producing well-researched, informative, and visually appealing content.

Engaging Titles and Thumbnails:
Craft attention-grabbing titles and design eye-catching thumbnails that entice viewers to click and read/watch.

Show Your Personality:
Let your personality shine through in your content. Be authentic and relatable to build a connection with your audience.

Build an Online Presence:
Establish a website or create a channel on platforms like YouTube or Vimeo. Optimize your profiles and bios to clearly convey your niche and what you offer.

SEO Optimization:
Learn about search engine optimization (SEO) to help your content rank higher on search engines. Incorporate fitting keywords, meta descriptions, and alternate text for images.

Engage with Your Audience:
Respond to comments, messages, and emails from your audience. Create a sense of community by valuing and interacting with your followers.

Networking:
Connect with fellow bloggers or vloggers in your niche. Collaborate on projects, cross-promote each other's content, and share insights.

Monetization Strategies:
Explore various monetization options, such as affiliate marketing, sponsored content, selling digital products, offering online courses, or using platforms like Patreon.

Consistency is Key:
Regularly update your blog or channel with fresh content. Consistency helps maintain your audience's interest and keeps them coming back for more.

Promotion:
Share your content on social media platforms and relevant online communities. Engage with your audience on these platforms to increase your reach.

Analytics and Insights:
Use analytics tools to track the performance of your content. Identify which topics or formats resonate the most with your audience and tailor your strategy accordingly.

Continuous Learning:
Stay up to date with industry trends, content creation techniques, and new platforms. Consistent learning ensures your content remains current and applicable.

Adapt and Evolve:
Be open to evolving your content strategy based on feedback and changing trends. Adaptability is crucial in the ever-changing world of online content.

Keep in mind that achieving success in blogging or vlogging requires patience. Focus on creating valuable content and building a loyal audience, and the rewards will come with persistence and dedication.

Fitness Coaching: Offer virtual fitness training sessions or create personalized workout plans

In an era where health and wellness take center stage, fitness coaching has emerged as a transformative profession. With the flexibility of virtual training sessions and personalized workout plans, fitness coaches empower individuals to achieve their health goals. This chapter serves as your roadmap to entering the world of fitness coaching, exploring its significance, benefits, strategies, and essential steps to build a thriving business.

Identify Your Niche:
Determine your fitness specialization. It could be anything from weight loss and strength training to yoga or specialized workouts for certain demographics (e.g., postnatal, seniors).

Certification and Education:
Gain the necessary fitness certifications and education to ensure you have the expertise to guide your clients safely and effectively.

Define Your Approach:
Develop a unique approach that sets you apart. Whether it's a specific training philosophy, a focus on mindset, or innovative workout techniques, differentiate yourself.

Online Presence:
Create a professional website showcasing your expertise, services, success stories, and contact information. Include a blog with fitness tips and informative articles.

Branding:
Develop a brand identity that reflects your style and values. Choose a memorable business name, design a logo, and create a consistent visual theme.

Content Creation:
Produce valuable content related to fitness and health. This could include workout videos, nutritional advice, motivational posts, and success stories.

Virtual Training Options:
Decide on the type of virtual services you'll offer—live training sessions, pre-recorded workouts, personalized training plans, or a combination.

Customized Plans:
If offering personalized training plans, analyze each client's goals, fitness level, and any limitations. Tailor workout and nutrition plans accordingly.

Virtual Platform:
Choose a reliable platform for virtual training sessions. Consider options like Zoom, Skype, or fitness-specific platforms with integrated features.

Safety First:
Emphasize the importance of proper form and technique to prevent injuries. Remind clients to consult a healthcare professional before beginning any new fitness program.

Progress Tracking:
Implement a system to track clients' progress. This could include regular assessments, before-and-after photos, or tracking software.

Engagement:
Stay engaged with clients through regular check-ins, messages, and emails. Offer support, motivation, and guidance to keep them on track.

Community Building:
Create an online community where clients can connect, share their progress, and support each other. This sense of community can boost motivation.

Pricing Strategy:
Determine your pricing model—session-based, monthly packages, or subscription-based for access to your content library.

Marketing:
Utilize social media platforms to showcase your expertise. Share workout tips, success stories, and behind-the-scenes glimpses of your fitness journey.

Client Testimonials:
Showcase success stories and testimonials from clients who have achieved their fitness goals with your guidance.

Collaborations:
Collaborate with nutritionists, wellness experts, or other fitness professionals to offer comprehensive services.

Feedback Loop:
Regularly gather feedback from clients to improve your services. Listen to their needs and adjust your offerings accordingly.

Ongoing Education:
Remain informed about the latest developments in fitness trends, research, and methods. Continuous learning will enhance your expertise.

Certifications:
Consider expanding your certifications to offer more specialized services and attract a broader clientele.

Passion and Patience:
Approach your coaching with passion and patience. Building a client base and seeing results takes time.

By combining your expertise, creativity, and a client-centered approach, you can establish a thriving fitness coaching business that helps clients achieve their health and fitness goals.

Cooking/Baking: Sell homemade meals, baked goods, or cooking classes online

The enticing aromas of homemade meals and freshly baked goods have the power to evoke nostalgia and create moments of joy. In the digital age, culinary enthusiasts have harnessed their passion for cooking and baking into profitable ventures. This chapter is your gateway to the culinary world of selling homemade meals, baked goods, and cooking classes online. Explore the significance, strategies, benefits, and key steps to establish a thriving cooking or baking business.

Culinary Expertise:
Leverage your cooking or baking skills and identify your specialty. It could be comfort food, healthy meals, international cuisine, or decadent desserts.

Legal Considerations:
Research local regulations and obtain any necessary licenses or permits for operating a food business from your home.

Unique Selling Point:
Define what sets your culinary offerings apart from others. It could be your secret family recipes, use of organic ingredients, or a creative twist on classic dishes.

Branding and Storytelling:
Develop a brand story that connects with your audience. Share the inspiration behind your dishes or your culinary journey.

Menu Creation:
Design a diverse menu that showcases your specialties. Offer a range of options, including vegetarian, vegan, gluten-free, and allergen-friendly choices.

Food Presentation:
Pay attention to food presentation. High-quality visuals can make your dishes more appealing and drive customer interest.

Pricing Strategy:
Calculate your costs, including ingredients, packaging, and overhead. Determine competitive pricing that mirrors the value you offer.

Packaging:
Invest in attractive and eco-friendly packaging that keeps your food fresh and presents it beautifully.

Online Platform:
Create a user-friendly website or use platforms like Etsy, Shopify, or social media to showcase your offerings, pricing, and ordering process.

Food Photography:
Capture mouthwatering photos of your dishes. Visuals play a crucial role in enticing customers to make a purchase.

Ordering System:
Set up a seamless ordering and payment system. Provide clear instructions for customers to place orders.

Delivery/Pickup Options:
Offer delivery or pickup options for your customers. Ensure that your food is delivered in a timely manner and remains fresh.

Customer Reviews:
Encourage customers to leave reviews and testimonials. Positive feedback can build trust and attract more customers.

Cooking Classes:
If offering cooking classes, create a schedule and curriculum. Develop engaging content, recipes, and interactive activities.

Virtual Cooking Classes:
Host online cooking classes via platforms like Zoom or YouTube Live. Share your knowledge, cooking techniques, and tips in an engaging way.

Ingredient Kits:
Offer ingredient kits for your cooking classes. Package and deliver pre-measured ingredients to make it convenient for participants.

Engagement:
Engage with your audience on social media. Share cooking tips, behind-the-scenes glimpses, and stories about your culinary creations.

Seasonal Specials:
Introduce seasonal or holiday-themed dishes and promotions to attract a wider audience.

Collaborations:
Collaborate with local farmers, suppliers, or other food businesses to source high-quality ingredients and expand your reach.

Feedback and Improvement:
Continuously gather feedback from customers and participants. Use their input to refine your offerings and enhance the customer experience.

Continuous Learning:
Stay updated with culinary trends, techniques, and food safety practices. Invest in your professional development.

Passion and Dedication:
Approach your cooking/baking business with passion and dedication. Your love for food will shine through and attract customers who share your enthusiasm.

By blending your culinary skills with creativity, innovation, and a commitment to quality, you can build a successful cooking/baking business that delights taste buds and leaves a lasting impression on your customers.

Digital Marketing Consultancy: Help businesses improve their online presence and marketing strategies

In the digital age, a strong online presence is paramount for businesses seeking growth and success. Digital marketing consultancies have emerged as trusted advisors, offering expertise to enhance online visibility and craft effective marketing strategies. This article is your roadmap to venturing into the realm of digital marketing consultancy, exploring its significance, benefits, strategies, and crucial steps to establish a thriving consultancy business.

Self-Assessment:
Evaluate your digital marketing skills and identify your areas of expertise, whether it's social media, SEO, content marketing, or paid advertising.

Niche Selection:
Choose a specific industry or niche to focus on. Specializing can make you a go-to expert in that field and help you stand out.

Business Plan:
Develop a comprehensive business plan that outlines your target market, services, pricing structure, marketing strategies, and growth goals.

Branding and Website:
Create a professional brand identity, including a logo and color scheme. Develop a user-friendly website that showcases your services, case studies, and client testimonials.

Portfolio:
Build a portfolio of past projects, highlighting successful campaigns, increased website traffic, or improved ROI for your clients.

Networking:
Attend industry events, webinars, and conferences to network with potential clients and stay updated with the latest trends.

Content Creation:
Start a blog or produce valuable content related to digital marketing. This showcases your expertise and attracts potential clients through organic search.

Social Media Presence:
Build a robust presence on social media platforms pertinent to your intended audience. Share insightful content, engage with your audience, and position yourself as an authority.

Client Outreach:
Reach out to businesses in your niche through email, social media, or networking events. Tailor your pitch to their specific pain points and needs.

Initial Assessments:
Offer free initial consultations to understand potential clients' current strategies and challenges. Provide a high-level assessment and suggest potential solutions.

Customized Strategies:
Create tailored digital marketing strategies for each client. Address their unique goals, target audience, and budget.

Execution and Monitoring:
Implement the strategies you've developed. Monitor and analyze key performance indicators (KPIs) to measure success and make data-driven adjustments.

Clear Communication:
Maintain open communication with your clients. Provide regular updates on progress and results to ensure transparency.

Continuous Learning:
Stay updated with the ever-evolving world of digital marketing. Master new platforms, tools, and tactics to offer the best solutions to your clients.

Collaborations:
Partner with other marketing professionals, designers, or developers to offer comprehensive solutions to your clients.

Client Education:
Empower your clients by educating them about digital marketing concepts. This fosters trust and helps them understand the value you provide.

Case Studies and Testimonials:
Showcase success stories and testimonials from satisfied clients on your website and marketing materials.

Upselling:
As you build trust with clients, identify additional services or opportunities for improvement. Upselling can lead to ongoing work and increased revenue.

Feedback Loop:
Regularly gather feedback from clients to ensure their needs are being met and to refine your services.

Results-Oriented Approach:
Focus on delivering tangible results that positively impact your clients' businesses. This builds your reputation and generates referrals.

By combining your expertise, creativity, and client-centered approach, you can establish a successful digital marketing consultancy that helps businesses thrive in the digital landscape.

Online Coaching: Offer life coaching, career guidance, or personal development services

In a world that values personal and professional growth, online coaching has emerged as a powerful way to guide individuals toward success. Online coaching offers personalized support, helping clients navigate life's challenges, define their goals, and unleash their full potential. This article serves as your roadmap to entering the world of online coaching, exploring its significance, benefits, strategies, and essential steps to build a thriving coaching business.

Identify Your Niche:
Determine the specific area of coaching you're passionate about, whether it's life coaching, career guidance, mindset coaching, wellness coaching, or personal development.

Skills and Credentials:
Acquire the necessary coaching skills and, if applicable, certifications or training. Building credibility is important in the coaching industry.

Define Your Approach:
Develop a unique coaching philosophy or approach that reflects your values and resonates with your potential clients.

Target Audience:
Identify the type of individuals you want to work with. Tailor your coaching services to their needs and aspirations.

Brand Identity:
Create a brand identity that represents your coaching style and values. Choose a memorable business name, design a logo, and maintain a consistent visual theme.

Online Presence:
Build a professional website that showcases your coaching services, your expertise, client testimonials, and your contact information.

Content Creation:
Share valuable content through blog posts, videos, or podcasts related to your coaching niche. This showcases your proficiency and draws potential customers.

Social Media Engagement:
Develop a strong presence on social media platforms that your target audience frequents. Share insightful content, engage with your audience, and provide value.

Client Outreach:
Reach out to potential clients through social media, networking events, or webinars. Offer free resources or assessments to initiate contact.

Initial Consultations:
Offer free initial consultations to understand potential clients' goals and challenges. Provide a taste of your coaching approach and suggest how you can help.

Customized Coaching Plans:
Develop personalized coaching plans tailored to each client's needs and goals. Outline the structure, sessions, and goals of the coaching relationship.

Virtual Sessions:
Host online coaching sessions via video conferencing platforms like Zoom or Skype. Create a comfortable and private environment for meaningful discussions.

Goal Setting:
Collaboratively set clear and achievable goals with your clients. Break down larger goals into smaller steps for a sense of progress.

Accountability:
Provide accountability and support to help your clients stay motivated and focused on their objectives.

Feedback and Reflection:
Encourage clients to reflect on their progress between sessions. Use feedback to adjust coaching strategies and approaches.

Tools and Resources:
Recommend books, worksheets, exercises, or other resources that align with your coaching philosophy and support your clients' growth.

Continuous Learning:
Stay updated with the latest coaching techniques, methodologies, and personal development trends. Invest in your professional development.

Empower Clients:
Empower clients by helping them uncover their strengths, overcome challenges, and tap into their potential.

Confidentiality:
Emphasize the importance of confidentiality in your coaching relationship. Clients should feel safe discussing personal matters.

Progress Tracking:
Develop a system for tracking client progress and milestones. Celebrate successes together.

Payment Structure:
Determine your pricing structure—session-based, package-based, or subscription-based—and communicate it clearly to clients.

Mindful Listening:
Practice active and mindful listening during coaching sessions. Show empathy, validate feelings, and ask thought-provoking questions.

By blending your coaching skills with creativity, empathy, and a genuine desire to help clients reach their goals, you can establish a thriving online coaching business that empowers individuals to transform their lives.

Handmade Crafts: Create and sell crafts, jewelry, or art through online marketplaces

In a world driven by mass production, the allure of handmade crafts stands strong. Crafting offers a medium of artistic expression, and with the rise of online marketplaces, artisans have found a platform to showcase and sell their unique creations. This chapter serves as your compass to navigate the world of handmade crafts, exploring its significance, strategies, benefits, and essential steps to establish a thriving crafts business online.

Craft Specialization:
Identify the type of crafts you excel in, whether it's jewelry, ceramics, candles, knitwear, or any other craft.

Unique Selling Point:
Define what sets your handmade crafts apart. It could be your use of sustainable materials, intricate designs, or a distinctive style.

Skill Refinement:
Continuously refine your crafting skills through practice, workshops, and experimenting with new techniques.

Materials Sourcing:
Source high-quality materials that align with your craft and brand values. Consider eco-friendly options if applicable.

Crafting Space:
Set up a well-organized crafting space with proper lighting, storage, and tools.

Branding and Storytelling:
Develop a brand story that reflects your journey as a crafter. Share the inspiration behind each piece to connect with customers.

Craft Photography:
Invest in high-quality photography to showcase your crafts. Visual appeal plays a huge role in attracting buyers.

Craft Packaging:
Design appealing packaging that protects your crafts and enhances the unboxing experience for customers.

Online Presence:
Create an online store on platforms like Etsy, Shopify, or your own website. Feature your crafts with clear descriptions and pricing.

Social Media:
Establish a strong social media presence. Share behind-the-scenes glimpses, work-in-progress shots, and engage with your audience.

Craft Tutorials:
Share craft tutorials or DIY guides related to your craft on platforms like YouTube or your blog. This positions you as an expert.

Customer Interaction:
Engage with customers through comments, messages, and emails. Personalized communication builds a loyal customer base.

Pricing Strategy:
Calculate the cost of materials, labor, and overhead to set competitive prices. Ensure your pricing reflects the quality and value of your crafts.

Limited Editions:
Offer limited-edition or one-of-a-kind pieces to create a sense of exclusivity and urgency among buyers.

Craft Fairs and Markets:
Participate in local craft fairs, markets, or exhibitions to showcase your crafts and connect with potential customers.

Collaborations:
Collaborate with other artisans or artists for cross-promotion or joint projects that expand your reach.

Customer Feedback:
Encourage buyers to leave reviews and testimonials. Positive feedback builds credibility and trust.

Seasonal and Trend-Based Crafts:
Introduce crafts inspired by seasons or current trends. This keeps your offerings fresh and relevant.

Subscription Boxes:
Offer a subscription box service featuring a selection of your crafts each month. This generates recurring revenue.

Craft Workshops:
Host online or offline craft workshops to teach others your craft techniques. This diversifies your income streams.

Bulk Orders:
Cater to bulk orders for corporate gifts, weddings, or special occasions. Customization options can attract business clients.

Continuous Learning:
Stay updated with crafting trends, new techniques, and innovations in your craft niche.

Ethical Practices:
If relevant, communicate your commitment to ethical sourcing, sustainability, and eco-friendly practices.

By blending your crafting skills with creativity, attention to detail, and a passion for creating beautiful pieces, you can establish a successful handmade crafts business that resonates with buyers and adds beauty to their lives.

App Development: If you have coding skills, create and sell mobile apps

In the digital age, mobile apps have become integral to modern life, transforming the way we communicate, work, and entertain. If you possess coding skills and a passion for technology, starting an app development business offers a rewarding opportunity to create innovative solutions for diverse needs. This chapter serves as your roadmap to navigate the realm of app development, exploring its significance, strategies, benefits, and essential steps to establish a thriving app development business.

Skill Assessment:
Evaluate your coding skills and proficiency in app development. Identify the platforms you're comfortable working with (iOS, Android, cross-platform).

Niche Selection:
Decide on the type of apps you want to develop—games, productivity tools, e-commerce, health, education, or any other category.

Market Research:
Research the app market to identify trends, user needs, and gaps that your apps could fill.

Unique Value Proposition:
Define what makes your apps unique. It could be innovative features, user-friendly interface, or solving a specific problem.

Idea Generation:
Brainstorm app ideas that align with your skills and market demand. Consider how your apps can provide value to users.

Prototyping and Design:
Create wireframes and prototypes to visualize the app's user interface and functionality. Create an interface that is visually attractive and user-friendly.

Coding and Development:
Write the code for your app, ensuring it functions smoothly, esponds quickly, and is optimized for performance.

Testing Phase:
Thoroughly test your app to identify and fix bugs, glitches, and user experience issues.

User Feedback:
Gather feedback from beta testers or potential users to make improvements and enhancements.

Monetization Strategy:
Decide how you'll monetize your app—through upfront purchase, in-app purchases, subscriptions, ads, or a combination.

App Store Guidelines:
Familiarize yourself with the guidelines of app stores (App Store, Google Play) to ensure your app meets their standards.

App Store Optimization (ASO):
Optimize your app's title, description, keywords, and screenshots to improve its visibility and discoverability on app stores.

App Marketing:
Develop a marketing plan to promote your app. Utilize social media, content marketing, influencer partnerships, and press releases.

Landing Page:
Create a professional landing page for your app with details, screenshots, and a call to action for users to download.

App Launch:
Launch your app with a marketing campaign. Leverage social media, email marketing, and targeted advertisements.

User Support: Provide customer support to address user inquiries, feedback, and issues promptly.

App Updates:
Continuously improve your app based on user feedback and evolving technology trends. Regular updates keep users engaged.

Analytics and Insights:
Implement analytics tools to track user behavior, engagement, and other metrics. Use data to make informed decisions.

Pricing Strategy:
Set competitive pricing for your app based on its features, value, and the market.

App Security:
Prioritize app security to protect user data and provide a safe experience.

Networking:
Connect with other app developers, attend industry events, and join online communities to stay informed and exchange insights.

Continuous Learning:
Stay updated with the latest coding languages, frameworks, and best practices in app development.

App Portfolio:
Showcase your app portfolio on a professional website or portfolio platform to demonstrate your expertise.

By combining your coding skills with creativity, problem-solving, and dedication, you can establish a successful app development business that provides innovative solutions and adds value to users' digital experiences.

Pet Services: Offer pet sitting, dog walking, or grooming services

In a world where pets are beloved members of the family, the demand for professional pet services is on the rise. Offering pet owners peace of mind and their furry friends a dose of TLC, pet services encompass a range of offerings, from pet sitting to dog walking and grooming. This chapter serves as your roadmap to entering the world of pet services, exploring its significance, strategies, benefits, and essential steps to establish a thriving business catering to our four-legged companions.

Pet Services Niche:
Decide on the specific pet services you'll offer—pet sitting, dog walking, grooming, or a combination.

Passion for Pets:
Show your genuine love for animals, as clients will trust you more if they see your passion.

Skills and Knowledge:
Acquire necessary skills, knowledge, and possibly certifications for pet care and grooming.

Legal Requirements:
Research and adhere to local regulations, licenses, and insurance needed for operating a pet services business.

Branding:
Develop a brand identity that reflects your care and professionalism. Choose a business name, design a logo, and create a consistent visual theme.

Online Presence:
Create a user-friendly website showcasing your services, pricing, service areas, and contact details.

Service Packages:
Create different service packages to cater to varying needs and budgets of pet owners.

Safety Measures:
Implement strict safety protocols to ensure the well-being of the pets in your care.

Client Communication:
Establish open communication with pet owners. Provide regular updates, photos, and feedback on their pets' well-being.

Pet-Friendly Space:
If offering services like pet sitting, ensure you have a pet-friendly space in your home or a designated area.

Pet Walking Routes:
Plan safe and enjoyable walking routes for dogs. Consider parks, trails, and pet-friendly areas.

Grooming Supplies:
Invest in high-quality grooming supplies and equipment if offering grooming services.

Marketing Materials:
Design and distribute flyers, business cards, and promotional materials in local pet stores or community centers.

Social Media:
Share photos and stories of the pets you care for on social media. Engage with pet-loving audiences to build a following.

Testimonials:
Gather testimonials from satisfied clients and showcase them on your website and marketing materials.

Pet Safety Training:
Educate yourself on pet safety, CPR, and first aid. This builds trust with pet owners.

Unique Offerings:
Introduce unique offerings, such as themed grooming sessions or personalized pet sitting experiences.

Networking: Collaborate with local veterinarians, pet stores, and animal shelters to expand your network.

Educational Content:
Share informative content about pet care, grooming tips, or behavior advice to position yourself as an expert.

Community Involvement:
Participate in community events, fairs, or pet expos to promote your services and connect with pet owners.

Flexible Hours:
Offer flexible hours to accommodate clients' schedules, especially if you're offering services like pet sitting.

Extras:
Consider offering add-on services like pet photography, pet transportation, or even organizing pet playdates.
Consistency:
Provide consistent and reliable services to build trust with clients and their pets.

Continuous Learning:
Stay updated on the latest trends and practices in pet care and grooming through workshops and courses.

By blending your love for animals with professionalism, safety measures, and a personalized approach, you can create a successful pet services business that pet owners can trust and rely on.

Online Reselling: Source and sell products from thrift stores or wholesalers on platforms like Amazon

In a world driven by e-commerce and consumerism, the practice of online reselling has gained momentum as a lucrative venture. With platforms like Amazon providing a global stage, individuals can source products from thrift stores, wholesalers, or even their own closets to resell to a vast audience. This chapter serves as your guide to entering the world of online reselling, exploring its significance, strategies, benefits, and essential steps to establish a thriving reselling business.

Niche Selection:
Identify a specific niche or category of products you're interested in reselling, whether it's clothing, electronics, home decor, vintage items, or a unique theme.

Market Research:
Research demand and trends within your chosen niche. Understand what products sell well and at what price points.

Sourcing Strategy:
Determine your sourcing strategy—thrift stores, garage sales, wholesalers, clearance sales, or a combination of sources.

Quality Control:
Focus on sourcing high-quality products in good condition. Ensure that items are clean, functional, and well-preserved.

Competitive Pricing:
Price your products competitively, considering your costs, market value, and potential profit margin.

Product Photography:
Allocate effort to capture product images of superior quality. Clear, well-lit images help attract buyers.

Listing Optimization:
Write compelling and detailed product descriptions. Use relevant keywords to improve your products' visibility in search results.

Online Selling Platforms:
Choose online platforms for selling, such as Amazon, eBay, Etsy, or dedicated niche marketplaces.

Account Setup:
Create professional seller accounts on your chosen platforms. Fill out all necessary information accurately.

Shipping and Packaging:
Determine your shipping methods and packaging. Consider offering free or discounted shipping to attract buyers.

Branding:
Develop a brand name, logo, and visual identity that sets you apart in the online marketplace.

Inventory Management:
Manage your inventory by monitoring stock levels to prevent over-sales or stock depletion.

Customer Service:
Provide excellent customer service, respond promptly to inquiries, and address any issues professionally.

Shipping Logistics:
Decide whether you'll handle shipping yourself or use fulfillment services like Amazon FBA for convenience.

Returns and Refunds:
Set clear policies for returns and refunds. Make the process hassle-free for buyers.

Marketing Strategies:
Utilize social media, content marketing, and email campaigns to promote your products and engage with potential customers.

Sales Optimization:
Continuously monitor your sales performance. Experiment with different pricing strategies, promotions, and listings to optimize your sales.

Customer Reviews:
Motivate purchasers to share reviews following their transactions. Positive reviews build credibility and trust.

Adapt to Trends:
Stay updated with industry trends, seasonal demands, and popular products in your niche.

Continuous Learning:
Stay informed about best practices, changes in platform policies, and emerging market trends.

Networking:
Connect with other resellers, attend online reselling events, and join online communities to share insights.

Financial Management:
Keep accurate records of your expenses, profits, and taxes. Good financial management is essential for long-term success.

Sustainability:
Consider incorporating sustainable practices, such as eco-friendly packaging or sourcing from ethical suppliers.

By combining your sourcing skills, creativity, and business acumen, you can build a thriving online reselling business that provides value to buyers while generating profits for you.

Gardening/Landscaping: Provide gardening advice, plant sales, or landscape design services

In a world where green spaces bring tranquility and beauty to urban landscapes, the gardening and landscaping industry offers a realm of creativity and serenity. Whether providing gardening advice, selling plants, or designing breathtaking landscapes, this business avenue blends nature with entrepreneurship. This article serves as your guide to entering the realm of gardening and landscaping, exploring its significance, strategies, benefits, and essential steps to establish a thriving green-focused venture.

Passion and Knowledge:
Tap into your love for plants and gardening. Deepen your knowledge through research, courses, and hands-on experience.

Niche Identification:
Decide on your niche—garden design, plant sales, urban gardening, landscaping, or a combination.

Skills Development:
Develop skills in horticulture, landscaping design, and plant care techniques. Consider obtaining relevant certifications.

Market Research:
Understand your local market's gardening and landscaping needs. Identify gaps that your services can fill.

Portfolio Building:
Create a portfolio showcasing your gardening and landscaping projects. Include before-and-after photos and detailed case studies.

Garden Consultations:
Offer garden consultations where you assess clients' spaces, discuss their preferences, and provide tailored recommendations.

Design Services:
If offering landscape design services, create visually appealing and functional designs that match clients' visions.

Plant Selection:
Recommend suitable plant varieties based on clients' preferences, climate, and soil conditions.

Sourcing Plants:
Partner with local nurseries or growers to source high-quality plants for your clients.

Educational Workshops:
Host gardening workshops or webinars to educate clients and gardening enthusiasts about plant care, landscaping, and design.

Online Presence:
Build a professional website showcasing your services, portfolio, testimonials, and blog posts on gardening tips.

Content Creation:
Create engaging content like blog posts, videos, or infographics on gardening techniques, plant care, and design ideas.

Social Media Engagement:
Utilize platforms like Instagram, Pinterest, and Facebook to share your expertise, showcase your work, and connect with your audience.

Online Plant Sales:
If offering plant sales, set up an online shop with clear product descriptions, care instructions, and attractive visuals.

Branding and Logo:
Develop a brand identity that reflects your style and values. A memorable logo can enhance your brand recognition.

Local Networking:
Collaborate with local garden clubs, landscapers, and nurseries to expand your network and gain referrals.

Sustainable Practices:
Promote eco-friendly gardening practices and educate clients about sustainable landscaping options.

Interactive Designs:
Incorporate interactive elements like water features, seating areas, or edible gardens to create unique and engaging landscapes.

Quotes and Proposals:
Provide detailed quotes and proposals to clients, outlining the scope of work, timeline, and cost estimates.

Client Relationships:
Foster strong relationships with clients through clear communication, regular updates, and post-project follow-ups.

Seasonal Offerings:
Adapt your services to different seasons—spring planting, fall cleanups, winter landscaping planning, etc.

Testimonials and Reviews:
Showcase positive feedback from satisfied clients on your website and marketing materials.

Photography:
Capture high-quality photos of your gardening and landscaping projects. Visuals can speak volumes about your expertise.

Business Growth:
As your business grows, consider hiring additional staff or partnering with other experts in the field.

Feedback Loop:
Regularly gather feedback from clients to continuously improve your services and client experience.

Continuous Learning:
Stay updated with gardening trends, new plant varieties, sustainable landscaping practices, and design techniques.

By combining your gardening skills with creativity, knowledge, and a customer-centric approach, you can create a successful gardening and landscaping business that transforms outdoor spaces and brings joy to your clients' lives.

Home Cleaning Services: Offer cleaning and organizing services to local clients

In a world where time is precious and cleanliness is paramount, the demand for professional home cleaning and organizing services continues to rise. Offering individuals the gift of a clean and orderly living space, a home cleaning services business is an opportunity to create a positive impact and provide peace of mind. This chapter serves as your roadmap to entering the world of home cleaning services, exploring its significance, strategies, benefits, and essential steps to establish a thriving cleaning business.

Passion for Cleanliness:
Embrace your passion for cleanliness and organization. Your enthusiasm will reflect in your work.

Service Offering:
Define the scope of your services—regular cleaning, deep cleaning, organization, post-event cleanups, or customized packages.

Market Research:
Understand the demand for cleaning services in your local area. Identify your target audience—busy professionals, families, seniors, etc.

Competitor Analysis:
Research other local cleaning services to identify gaps, pricing strategies, and potential areas for differentiation.

Specialization:
Consider specializing in a niche, such as eco-friendly cleaning, pet-friendly cleaning, or using specific cleaning products.

Supplies and Equipment:
Invest in high-quality cleaning supplies, eco-friendly products, and equipment like vacuum cleaners, mops, and microfiber cloths.

Pricing Structure:
Determine your pricing structure based on factors like the size of the space, the level of cleaning required, and the frequency of service.

Online Presence:
Create a professional website that showcases your services, pricing, contact details, and customer testimonials.

Branding:
Develop a brand identity that reflects your commitment to cleanliness, professionalism, and reliability.

Safety Protocols:
Implement strict safety protocols, especially during the ongoing pandemic, to ensure the health of both your clients and your staff.

Booking System:
 Set up an easy-to-use online booking system that allows clients to schedule appointments and choose the services they need.

Customer Communication:
Maintain clear communication with clients before, during, and after the cleaning process. Keep them informed about progress.

Cleaning Checklist:
Develop a detailed cleaning checklist to ensure that each area of the home is thoroughly cleaned and nothing is missed.

Eco-Friendly Practices:
Emphasize eco-friendly cleaning practices using non-toxic, biodegradable products. This can attract environmentally-conscious clients.

Training:
Train your cleaning staff to uphold high cleaning standards, professionalism, and respect for clients' privacy.

Feedback Collection:
Gather feedback from clients after each cleaning session. Use their input to improve your services.

Regulars and One-Time Services:
Offer both regular cleaning plans for recurring clients and one-time cleaning services for special occasions.

Emergency Cleanups:
Provide emergency cleaning services for last-minute events or unexpected situations.

Referral Program:
Implement a referral program to incentivize satisfied clients to refer new customers.

Quality Assurance:
Conduct regular quality checks to ensure consistent service quality across different cleaning sessions.

Social Media Engagement:
Use platforms like Instagram, Facebook, and TikTok to showcase before-and-after photos, cleaning tips, and customer stories.

Local Networking:
Partner with local real estate agents, property managers, and event planners to gain referrals.

Client Loyalty:
Offer loyalty discounts or promotions to encourage repeat business from satisfied clients.

Professional Appearance:
Ensure your staff is well-groomed and dressed in branded uniforms to project professionalism.

Time Management:
Efficiently manage your cleaning schedule to ensure timely services and avoid overbooking.

Upselling Opportunities:
Offer additional services like closet organization, window cleaning, or refrigerator cleaning as upselling opportunities.

Continuous Learning:
Stay updated with the latest cleaning techniques, products, and industry trends.By blending your cleanliness expertise with professionalism, attention to detail, and excellent customer service, you can establish a successful home cleaning services business that creates a clean and organized haven for your clients.

Tech Support: Provide technical assistance to individuals or small businesses remotely

In an era dominated by technology, the need for reliable technical assistance has become more crucial than ever. Providing remote tech support offers a lifeline to individuals and small businesses navigating the complexities of digital systems. This article serves as your guide to entering the world of remote tech support, exploring its significance, strategies, benefits, and essential steps to establish a thriving tech support business.

Skill Assessment:
Evaluate your technical expertise and identify the areas you can provide assistance in—software troubleshooting, device setup, network issues, etc.

Service Offering:
Define the range of tech support services you'll offer. Consider both hardware and software support.

Niche Specialization:
Consider specializing in a particular niche, such as home automation, cybersecurity, or specific software platforms.

Market Research:
Research the demand for tech support services in your target market. Identify pain points and common issues people face.

Remote Tools:
Invest in remote access and troubleshooting tools that allow you to assist clients virtually.

Pricing Structure:
Determine your pricing model—hourly rates, subscription plans, or per-service fees. Make it transparent to clients.

Online Presence:
Build a professional website detailing your services, expertise, pricing, and contact information.

Branding:
Create a professional and approachable brand identity that reflects your reliability and technical skills.

Client Communication:
Maintain clear and friendly communication with clients. Explain technical concepts in a simple and understandable manner.

Marketing Strategies:
Utilize social media, content marketing, and targeted online ads to promote your services.

Educational Content:
Share tech tips, tutorials, and troubleshooting guides through blog posts or video content. Establish yourself as an expert.

Social Proof:
Display client testimonials and success stories on your website. Positive feedback builds trust.

Online Booking System:
Set up an online booking system where clients can schedule appointments for tech support.

Client Data Security:
Emphasize the security measures you take to protect clients' sensitive data during remote sessions.

Service Agreements:
Develop clear service agreements that outline the scope of work, terms of service, and client expectations.

Virtual Workshops:
Host virtual workshops or webinars on common tech topics to attract potential clients.

Networking:
Connect with local businesses, community centers, and organizations that might need your tech support services.

Customer Support:
Provide post-service support to address any follow-up questions or issues clients may have.

Problem-Solving Skills:
Hone your problem-solving skills to quickly diagnose and resolve tech issues.

Flexibility:
Offer flexible hours to accommodate clients' schedules, especially if you're dealing with small businesses.

Continuous Learning:
Stay updated with the latest tech trends, software updates, and troubleshooting techniques.

Online Reviews:
Encourage satisfied clients to leave online reviews on platforms like Google, Yelp, or social media.

Client Training:
Offer training sessions to help clients become more tech-savvy and confident in using their devices and software.

Upselling Opportunities:
Identify opportunities to upsell additional services like data backup, security audits, or software optimization.

Feedback Loop:
Regularly seek feedback from clients to improve your services and address any areas for enhancement.

By blending your technical skills with excellent customer service, communication, and a solution-oriented approach, you can create a successful tech support business that empowers individuals and small businesses to navigate the digital world with confidence.

Virtual Event Planning: Help plan and coordinate virtual events, conferences, or workshops

In a world where connections are forged through screens and gatherings take place in virtual spaces, the role of virtual event planners has become increasingly essential. Offering expertise in planning and coordinating virtual events, conferences, and workshops, this business avenue blends creativity with technology. This chapter serves as your roadmap to entering the world of virtual event planning, exploring its significance, strategies, benefits, and essential steps to establish a thriving event planning business in the digital realm.

Passion for Events:
Embrace your passion for creating memorable experiences and translating them into the virtual space.

Event Expertise:
Deepen your understanding of event planning by attending workshops, courses, and studying successful virtual events.

Niche Identification:
Decide on your niche—corporate events, webinars, virtual trade shows, workshops, or a specific industry.

Technology Familiarity:
Familiarize yourself with virtual event platforms, streaming technologies, and collaboration tools.

Client Consultation:
Offer free initial consultations to understand clients' objectives, target audience, and event goals.

Innovative Ideas:
 Brainstorm creative ideas to make virtual events engaging and interactive—gamification, networking sessions, live Q&A, etc.

Detailed Planning:
Develop detailed event plans, timelines, and budgets. Clearly outline each element of the event.

Vendor Relationships:
Build relationships with virtual event platform providers, tech support teams, graphic designers, and content creators.

Client Communication:
Maintain open communication with clients. Provide regular updates on event progress and involve them in decision-making.

Engaging Content:
Assist clients in creating compelling content—presentations, videos, graphics—that captivates virtual attendees.

Event Promotion:
Design marketing strategies to promote virtual events. Utilize social media, email campaigns, and partnerships.

Interactive Elements:
Incorporate interactive elements like polls, surveys, and live chat to engage attendees during virtual events.

Rehearsals:
Conduct thorough rehearsals with presenters and speakers to ensure smooth event execution.

Virtual Networking:
Plan virtual networking sessions or breakout rooms to facilitate connections among attendees.

Tech Support:
Provide real-time tech support during events to troubleshoot any technical glitches that arise.

Accessibility:
Ensure events are accessible to all attendees, considering different time zones and accessibility requirements.

Monetization Strategies:
Discuss potential monetization avenues—ticket sales, sponsorships, paid access to premium content.

Event Analytics:
Utilize event analytics to measure attendee engagement, session popularity, and overall event success.

Post-Event Engagement:
Plan post-event engagement strategies to maintain attendee interest and gather feedback.

Event Recording:
Offer options for event recording and on-demand access to extend the event's lifespan.

Client Testimonials:
Showcase positive feedback and testimonials from satisfied clients on your website and marketing materials.

Continuous Learning:
Stay updated with the latest virtual event trends, technology advancements, and engagement strategies.

Networking and Partnerships:
Collaborate with speakers, industry experts, and other event planners for joint events or cross-promotion.

Professional Development:
Attend industry webinars, conferences, and workshops to enhance your event planning skills.

Inclusivity:
Advocate for diverse representation among speakers and participants to create inclusive events.

Crisis Management:
Develop contingency plans to address unforeseen challenges and technical issues.

By blending your event planning skills with adaptability, creativity, and an understanding of virtual technology, you can establish a successful virtual event planning business that delivers seamless and engaging experiences for clients and attendees.

Personal Styling: Offer fashion advice and styling services through virtual consultations

In a world where fashion is a form of self-expression, personal stylists have emerged as guides on the journey to self-confidence and sartorial identity. Offering fashion advice and styling expertise through virtual consultations, this business avenue bridges the gap between individual tastes and current trends. This chapter serves as your guide to entering the realm of personal styling, exploring its significance, strategies, benefits, and essential steps to establish a thriving styling business in the digital age.

Fashion Passion:
Embrace your love for fashion, trends, and personal expression. Your enthusiasm will resonate with clients.

Fashion Expertise:
Deepen your knowledge of fashion by studying trends, styles, body types, and color theory.

Niche Selection:
Decide on your niche—casual wear, professional attire, special occasions, or a specific age group.

Client Consultations:
Offer virtual consultations to understand clients' style preferences, lifestyle, and fashion goals.

Body Type Analysis:
Help clients understand their body types and suggest clothing styles that flatter their shapes.

Closet Assessment:
Assist clients in assessing their current wardrobe. Identify pieces to keep, alter, or donate.

Virtual Shopping:
Curate virtual shopping lists based on clients' needs, preferences, and budget.

Mix and Match:
Teach clients how to mix and match existing pieces for versatile outfits.

Digital Lookbooks:
Create personalized digital lookbooks with outfit ideas and styling tips.

Color Coordination:
Advise clients on color coordination, helping them create cohesive and stylish outfits.

Virtual Fitting Room:
Recommend clothing items virtually by considering measurements and sizes.

Sustainable Fashion:
Introduce clients to sustainable fashion options, promoting conscious consumer choices.

Personalized Styling:
Tailor your styling advice to each client's unique personality and preferences.

Styling Tools:
Invest in fashion apps and styling tools that help visualize outfits and plan wardrobes.

Online Presence:
Develop a stylish website showcasing your services, portfolio, fashion tips, and client testimonials.

Branding:
Create a chic and visually appealing brand identity that reflects your fashion sense.

Social Media:
Use platforms like Instagram, Pinterest, and TikTok to share fashion tips, outfit ideas, and style inspiration.

Fashion Content:
Produce blog posts, videos, or podcasts on fashion trends, styling hacks, and industry insights.

Collaborations: Partner with fashion brands or local boutiques for cross-promotions and styling events.

Fashion Workshops:
Host virtual workshops on topics like capsule wardrobes, accessorizing, and creating themed looks.

Wardrobe Updates:
Provide clients with seasonal updates and suggestions for refreshing their wardrobes.

Client Transformation:
Showcase before-and-after transformations of clients' personal styles.

Confidence Building:
Help clients build confidence through their newfound sense of style.

Virtual Fashion Showcases:
Organize virtual fashion shows or style challenges to engage clients and showcase your skills.

Networking:
Connect with local fashion influencers, photographers, and makeup artists for collaborative projects.

Continual Learning:
Stay updated with the latest fashion trends, brands, and styling techniques.

Feedback Loop:
Regularly gather feedback from clients to refine your services and better meet their needs.

Inclusivity:
Ensure your styling services cater to diverse body types, genders, and styles.

Personal Growth:
Encourage clients to embrace fashion as a tool for personal growth and self-expression.

By combining your fashion flair with personalized attention, empathy, and creative styling solutions, you can establish a successful personal styling business that empowers clients to confidently express themselves through their wardrobes.

Remember to research your chosen idea, understand the market, and create a solid business plan before getting started.